YOUR WORLD THROUGH A
TELESCOPE

Silver Dolphin

Silver Dolphin

Silver Dolphin Books
An imprint of Printers Row Publishing Group
A division of Readerlink Distribution Services, LLC
10350 Barnes Canyon Road, Suite 100, San Diego, CA 92121
www.silverdolphinbooks.com

Copyright © 2020 Quarto Publishing plc.

Author: Nancy Dickmann
Consultant: David Hawksett
Illustrator: Nadene Naude/Beehive Art Agency and Norbert Sipos/Beehive Art Agency

All notations of errors or omissions should be addressed to Silver Dolphin Books, Editorial Department, at the above address. All other correspondence (author inquiries, permissions) concerning the content of this book should be addressed to:
Quarto Children's Books Ltd. an imprint of The Quarto Group.
The Old Brewery, 6 Blundell Street,London N7 9BH, United Kingdom.
www.quartoknows.com

ISBN: 978-1-64517-367-0

Manufactured, printed, and assembled in Shenzhen, China.
First printing, June 2020. HH/06/20

24 23 22 21 20   1 2 3 4 5

PICTURE CREDITS
t-top, b-bottom, l-left, r-right, c-centre, fc-front cover, bc-back cover
1l and 3l shutterstock/Cristian Cestaro, 1r, 3r and 21cl shutterstock/Pakhynushchy, 4b shutterstock/Ryan Fletcher, 6tl shutterstock/Brady Barrineau, 6r shutterstock/ Dominique landau, 6b and 7l shutterstock/Kolesove Sergei, 8l Pierre Borrel, 8c Adraen van de Venne, 8tr NASA/Justus Suttermans, 9t shutterstock/Georgios Kollidas, 10tl Pretzelpaws, 10r shutterstock/Lissandra Melo, 10c Jarek Tuszynski, 11cr NASA, 11br shutterstock/MarcelClemens, 19tl shutterstock/Arunsri Futemwong, 19cl shutterstock/Matt Gibson, 19r shutterstock/Anakumka, 19bl shutterstock/Wang LiQiang, 19br shutterstock/Nicolas Primola, 21bl shutterstock/Aluca69, 22–23 shutterstock/zhu difeng, 23tl shutterstock/Alizada Studios, 23cl shutterstock/James R. Martin, 23bl shutterstock/Gustavo Frazao, 23tr shutterstock/EastVillage Images, 24r shutterstock/Hampus design, 25tl shutterstock/NewAfrica, 25r shutterstock/ Alhovik, 25bl shutterstock/Georgii Shipin, 25br shutterstock/Georgios Kollidas, 26bl John T. Daniels, 27tl shutterstock/DimaBerlin, 27tr shutterstock/Rose Badasch, 27bl shutterstock/Ryan Fletcher, 27br shutterstock/Photos SS, 28bl shutterstock/peiyang, 28c and 30–31 shutterstock/Mike Ver Sprill, 30l shutterstock/EpicStockMedia, 30c shutterstock/Guppy2416, 31br shutterstock/dawool/Vector_dream_team/Anatolir/ fredrisher/Ksenica/peart, 32bl shutterstock/ManuMata, 33tr shutterstock/Procy, 33c, 33br, 37tr, 39b and 40bl NASA, 34–35 shutterstock/Castleski, 35b shutterstock/Chris Collins, 35br bigstock/Medardus, 37tl shutterstock/Targn Pleiades, 37b shutterstock/ Dotted Yeti, 39tr shutterstock/NASA/JPL/MSSS, 39cl shutterstock/Chrispo, 41tr shutterstock/Tristan3D, 41cr shutterstock/herlock_00, 41b shutterstock/David Hajnal, 42cl shutterstock/galsand, 43c shutterstock/Cristian Cestaro, 44–45 shutterstock/ oxameel, 47l shutterstock/Aliona Ursu, 47r shutterstock/Jurik Peter, 48tl shutterstock/DMstudio House, 49tr shutterstock/Wolfgang Kloehr, 51t shutterstock/ shooarts, 51c shutterstock/John A Davis, 52b shutterstock/Noah Sauve, 53c John Lanoue, 54t and 64 AstroBrallo 2011, 55t shutterstock/Maik Thomas, 55c shutterstock/Serrgey75, 55bl shutterstock/Albert Barr, 56bl ESA, 57c shutterstock/a. v. ley, 57b ESO/E.Slawik, 58, 59tl and 59tr NASA, 59bl shutterstock/Planet Delight, 61b shutterstock/Kostas Koutsaftikis,

YOUR WORLD THROUGH A
TELESCOPE

Silver Dolphin

CONTENTS

HOW A TELESCOPE WORKS

Your telescope lets you view things that are far away—but they will appear upside down! **Let's see how it works!**

Telescopes are truly amazing. They let us see faraway objects, sometimes in incredible detail. Telescopes can even peer into deep space! The simplest telescopes just need a rigid tube and two curved pieces of glass, called **lenses**, to magnify images.

HOW LENSES WORK

Light usually travels through the air in straight lines, but when it passes from one substance to another, such as from air into glass, it bends. This is called **refraction**. A **convex** lens is a piece of polished glass that is curved on both sides. The curves refract light when it passes through the lens. The rays of light bend so that they all come together (converge) at a single point beyond the other side of the lens, called the focal point. As the rays of light continue, they cross over to produce an upside-down image.

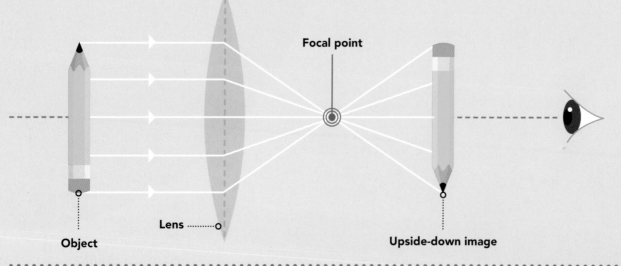

Focal point

Lens ·········o

Object

Upside-down image

SMALL AND FAR AWAY

If you and a friend are standing at opposite ends of a beach and your friend holds up a playing card, you won't be able to tell which card it is. From that distance, it's just too small. The lens in a telescope gathers more light from the card and creates a brighter image, making it clearer. But that's just the first step! For the second step, you need another lens.

WORKING IN PAIRS

A telescope has two lenses. The first is called the objective lens, and it is bigger. It gathers light from the object you are looking at and focuses it on a point inside the telescope (the focal point). The second lens, which is usually smaller, is called the **eyepiece** lens. It takes the bright light from the focal point of the objective lens and magnifies it. In effect, it spreads out the image so that it looks big.

Objective lens

Eyepiece lens

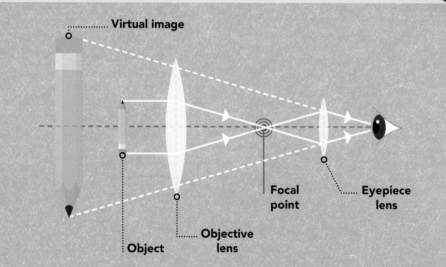

Virtual image

Focal point

Eyepiece lens

Object

Objective lens

PUTTING IT ALL TOGETHER

Together, the objective lens and the eyepiece lens are able to take in a lot of light, focus it into a point, then magnify the image in your vision. The size of the objective lens is called the telescope's **aperture**. The larger the aperture, the more light the telescope can collect and focus. This makes the final image brighter. The number of times the image is magnified depends on the shape of the eyepiece lens—the more rounded its shape, the greater it will magnify the image. However, the greater the magnification, the dimmer the image will be, so the eyepiece lens cannot be too curved. The tube holds the two lenses at the right distance from each other and keeps out any dust that would ruin the image.

HISTORY OF TELESCOPES

Ancient people studied the stars and planets, tracking their movements and looking for patterns. All they had to study them with was the naked eye, so these objects looked like pinpricks of light. No one realized that distant stars were just faraway versions of the Sun. The invention of the telescope changed that. This amazing tool allowed people to see faraway objects in detail, opening up a whole new world of knowledge.

LOOKING AT THE STARS

The Italian scientist Galileo Galilei soon heard about the new invention from a friend in Paris. He immediately realized how useful such a device would be for looking into space. Based on the description he had been given, he made his own version, which could magnify about 20 times. Galileo was the first person to point a telescope into space. He saw the **Moon**'s craters in detail, and in 1610, he discovered four moons **orbiting** Jupiter.

WHO WAS FIRST?

An eyeglasses-maker named Hans Lippershey applied for the first telescope patent in 1608. He lived in Middelburg in the Netherlands, which was known as a center for lens-making. (Another man from the same town, Zacharias Janssen, had invented the microscope several years earlier.) Lippershey was an expert in grinding lenses, and his device could magnify objects so that they appeared to be three times bigger. He called it a *kijker*, which means "looker" in Dutch.

AN EXCITING NEW TOY?

At least one other lens-maker came up with a similar idea around the same time as Lippershey. The Dutch government didn't grant either of them a patent because the device was too easy to copy. However, they paid Lippershey to make several copies of the invention. One was given to the king of France! The *kijker* was a novelty, but it had military uses, too. It allowed generals and ship captains to get a better view of their enemies.

QUICK FACT

Lippershey called his invention the "Dutch perspective glass"—not very catchy! It was first called a telescope, from the Greek for "far seeing," in 1611.

THE LIMITS OF VISION

The type of telescope used by Lippershey and Galileo is called a refractor because the lenses refract, or bend, light. These telescopes were limited by the size of the objective lens. To see really dim, faraway objects, a big objective lens is needed. But big lenses are heavy, which makes the telescope hard to hold steady. It is also very hard to make big lenses without flaws that ruin the image.

Galileo presents his telescope to the Pope.

USING MIRRORS

The famous English scientist Sir Isaac Newton solved the problem of lens size in 1668, when he invented the first **reflecting telescope**. Instead of passing through an objective lens, light traveled directly into a wide tube and bounced off a curved mirror at the bottom. The mirror had a **concave** shape—thicker on the sides than in the middle. It focused the reflected light onto a smaller, flat mirror, which bounced it into a magnifying eyepiece on the side of the telescope.

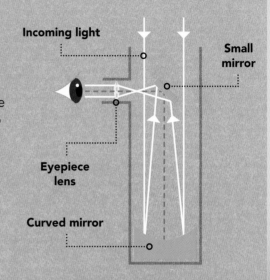

Incoming light

Small mirror

Eyepiece lens

Curved mirror

REFLECTING TELESCOPE

QUICK FACT

While observing Jupiter's moons in 1612, Galileo spotted Neptune. However, he believed that it was a faint star, and Neptune was not recognized as a planet until 1846.

MODERN TELESCOPES

Over the years, telescopes have become bigger and bigger. By the late 1600s, some refracting telescopes were more than 100 feet long! Since then, better mirrors and lenses have allowed **astronomers** to see more than ever before. In the twentieth century, new telescopes were developed to capture forms of invisible energy such as radio waves.

OBSERVATORIES

By the start of the twentieth century, scientists were using giant telescopes in special buildings called **observatories**. These observatories were often built in places far from cities, where dark skies were guaranteed. The best locations were high up on hills where the air is thinner and there is less distortion from currents of moving air. These observatories were often dome-shaped, with a slit in the roof that could be rotated to observe in any direction.

Lowell Observatory
in Arizona

Early radio telescope

NEW WAYS OF "SEEING"

Up to the 1930s, all telescopes were optical telescopes, which means they operated using visible light. Objects also give off other forms of energy that we cannot see, such as heat, radio waves, and gamma rays. Once astronomers realized this, they began building new devices to capture these other forms of energy. The first was the radio telescope, which was invented in 1932. It detected invisible radio waves given off by distant stars and galaxies. Today, the largest radio telescope is more than 1,500 feet wide.

QUICK FACT

Radio telescopes look very different from optical telescopes. The first radio telescope was an arrangement of poles and wires. Later ones used huge dishes to gather and focus the radio waves.

ENERGY WAVES

Energy travels in waves of radiation. The type of energy depends on the distance between each wave, called the **wavelength**. This type of energy ranges from gamma rays with wavelengths just billionths of an inch long to radio waves whose wavelengths are many feet long. Visible light lies in between these extremes. The range of wavelengths is known as the electromagnetic spectrum.

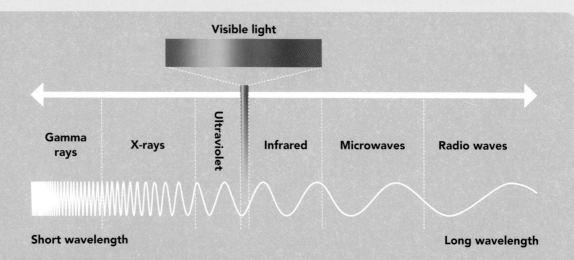

Visible light

Gamma rays

X-rays

Ultraviolet

Infrared

Microwaves

Radio waves

Short wavelength

Long wavelength

The Lovell Telescope, a radio telescope at Jodrell Bank Observatory in England

TELESCOPES IN SPACE

Earth is surrounded by a blanket of gases called the **atmosphere**. The gases keep Earth's temperature fairly steady and protect us from dangerous radiation from the Sun. However, they also block a lot of the energy that astronomers are interested in observing. To get a better view, astronomers have put telescopes in space. These remote-controlled telescopes are launched on rockets, and they stay in orbit around Earth, outside its atmosphere. Below are a few of the most important ones.

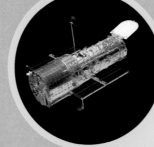

The Sun in ultraviolet

The Hubble Space Telescope

Telescope:	Launch date:	Type of energy it detects:
Hubble	1990	infrared, visible light, ultraviolet
Chandra	1999	X-rays
Spitzer	2003	infrared
Fermi	2008	gamma rays

BUILD YOUR TELESCOPE

Your telescope will give you a whole new view of your world and the universe, but you will need to be very careful. Even the smallest movement can mess up your view. Take your time putting the telescope pieces together and be careful not to bend parts or force pieces together.

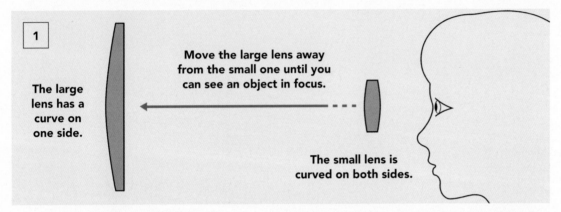

First, you need to check that your lenses are the right way around. To do this, hold them in front of your eyes, with the large lens in front of the smaller lens. Make sure that the curved side of the large lens is facing away from you. Look through the small lens and move the large lens backward and forward until you can focus on a distant object. If you can't focus on that object, turn the small lens around and try this again. When you can focus on a distant object, make a note of which way round the lenses were.

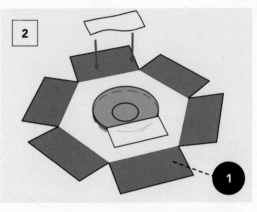

Place the small lens on top of part 1—make sure that you center it using the dashed red line. Add two small pieces of sticky tape to the top and bottom of the lens to hold it in place.

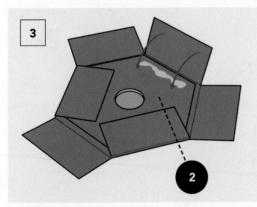

Place part 2 on top of the lens. Apply some glue to every other tab on part 1, then fold them over and stick them to the surface of part 2. Or you could use some sticky tape to hold them in place

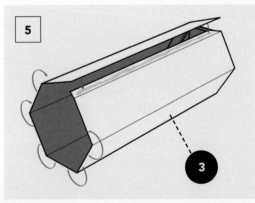

Apply a small amount of glue to one of the remaining three tabs on your lens holder and fix this tab onto one of the white spaces on the black side of part 3, as shown. Wait for the glue to dry.

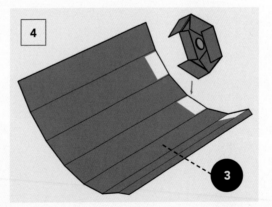

Roll part 3 around the lens holder, gluing the other tabs into place one at a time. Then glue the long tab on part 3 to complete the back tube.

6

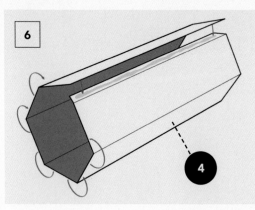

Roll part 4 along the folds and glue the long tab in place to make the middle tube.

4

7

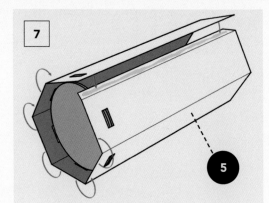

Place the larger lens into one of the slots on part 5 with the curved face of the lens facing out. Roll part 5 along the folds and glue the long tab in place to form the front tube. The lens should be held in place by the slots.

5

8

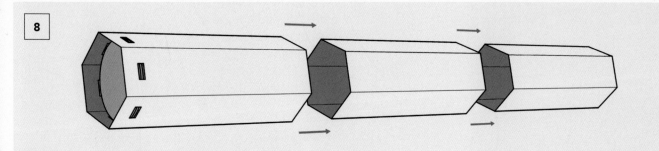

Once the glue has completely dried, slide the three tubes together—front, middle, and back—making sure that the lenses are at either end to complete your telescope.

HOW TO USE YOUR TELESCOPE

The front lens of your telescope collects light from distant objects, while the back lens focuses light rays to create a sharp image. Use the star maps in this book to locate the part of the sky you want to study and point your telescope in that direction. You may need to search carefully in order to find the object you want to study. Try to hold your telescope steady. You may want to lean against something to stay as still as possible.

Move the back tube in and out to focus the upside-down image of the object and make it as sharp as possible. You may need an adult to help you do this, if the telescope is too long.

Never look directly at the Sun as this could permanently damage your eyesight!

BUILD YOUR PLANETARIUM

Create your very own planetarium and shine the constellations of the night sky onto your bedroom walls and ceiling. Make sure that all the tabs are pushed firmly into the slots so that no light can sneak out through any gaps.

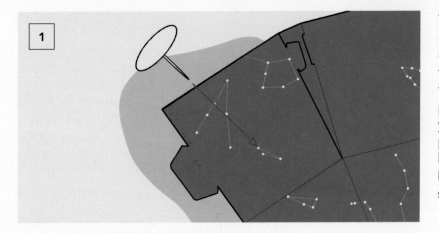

1

When you have pressed out your planetarium pieces, have an adult help you carefully push a thumbtack through each of the constellation points to make holes through which your stars will shine. Use a piece of modeling clay under each piece so you don't damage anything beneath when pushing the thumbtack through. You may have to repeat this process when the model has been made, as the tabs may obscure some of the holes.

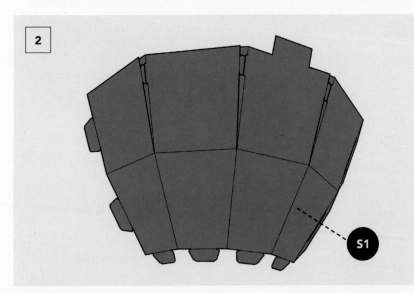

2

Fold along the edges and tabs of part S1. Carefully separate the lower panels from each other.

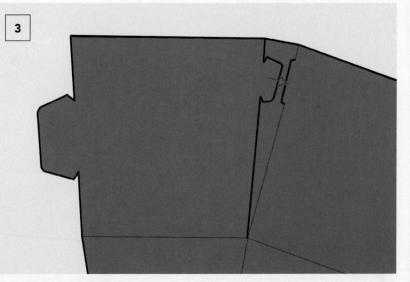

3

One by one, push the inner tabs on the lower panels into the slots next to them. As a result, S1 should become rounded.

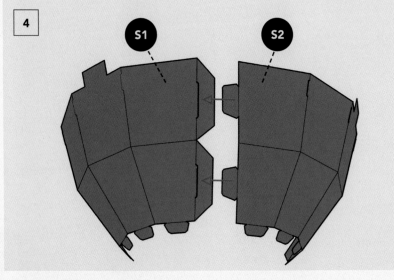

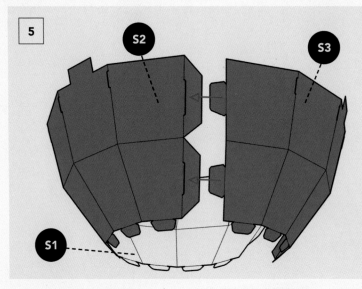

Repeat steps 2 and 3 on part S2, then slot the tabs on the side of S2 into slots on the side of S1.

Repeat steps 2 and 3 on part S3, then slot the tabs on the side of S3 into slots on the side of S2.

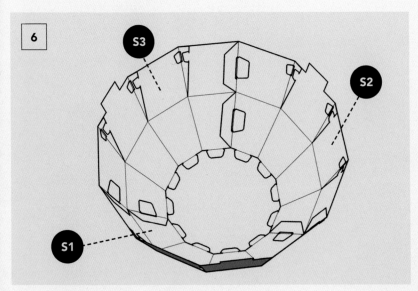

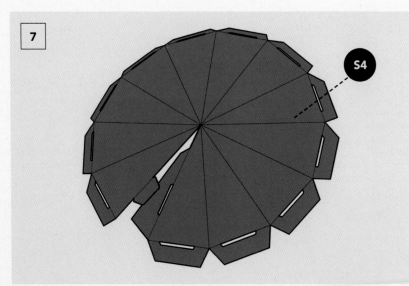

Join parts S3 and S1 using their tabs and slots to form a whole hemisphere ring.

Take part S4, and fold along its edges and tabs. Push the tab on the inner edge into the slot next to it, making a shallow dome.

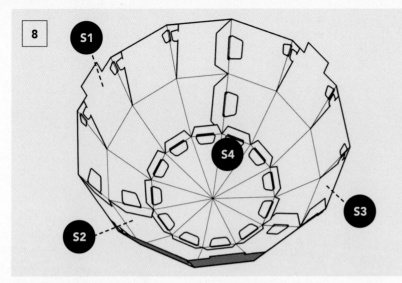

8

Line up the two red dots beneath parts S4 and S1, and slot the tabs along the tops of S1, S2, and S3 into the slots on S4 to complete the Southern Hemisphere. Repeat steps 2–8, but using parts N1–N4, to complete the Northern Hemisphere.

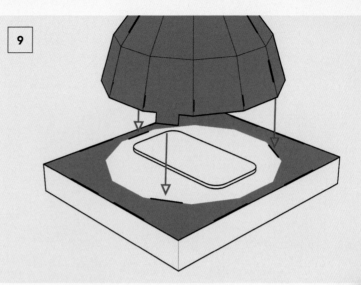

9

To illuminate your planetarium, turn on the light on your cell phone and place the phone on top of the tray, inside the marked area. Then put one of the hemispheres over your phone, pushing its tabs into the slots in the tray.

STAR MAPS

Because Earth is round, only half the sky is visible from your position. From the southern hemisphere you see stars that are never visible from the north, and vice versa. To chart the night sky we need two maps—one for the north and one for the south.

THE MILKY WAY

The paler ribbons show the disk of our own galaxy, though in fact all the stars shown on these maps are part of the Milky Way. The Milky Way appears thickest in the constellation Sagittarius, because the bulge in the center of the galaxy lies in this direction.

SOUTHERN

Many astronom southern skies because there of bright stars the sky. Instead hemisphere othe called Crux for as the Southe flags of se

NORTHERN HEMISPHERE

SOUTHERN HEMISPHERE

HOW TO USE YOUR PLANETARIUM

Make sure the room your hemisphere is in is nice and dark so that you can see the stars as clearly as possible. The light from your cell phone will shine through the holes in your planetarium dome, projecting the "stars" onto your walls and ceiling. See if you can identify which stars form each constellation. You can use your star maps to help you with this.

Move your planetarium closer or farther away from your walls and ceiling to sharpen the image of any constellation.

When you've studied the constellations on one hemisphere, swap the domes to see how the night sky appears on the other side of the world.

WATCHING WILDLIFE

While Galileo pointed his telescope into space, telescopes were also used on land and at sea. People still use telescopes to get an in-depth look at many types of animals, particularly birds. These fluttery creatures are wary of humans and have a habit of staying far away, making it difficult to get a good look at them...unless you have a telescope, of course!

BIRDS

Birds range in size from tiny wrens to enormous ostriches. All birds have wings, and many of them can fly, though others are unable to get off the ground. A bird's body is covered in feathers, and it has a bony beak or bill for a mouth. They are warm-blooded and produce young by laying eggs. All birds have two legs, but their legs and feet can look very different—some have long legs for wading, while others have short legs and feet that they use to perch on branches.

DINOSAURS IN YOUR BACKYARD

Did you know that birds are actually dinosaurs? For a long time, scientists knew that birds and dinosaurs had many similarities. Recently, new fossil finds have shown that birds are just another branch of the dinosaur family. Birds are the only type of dinosaur to survive when the rest were wiped out about 66 million years ago.

GET SPOTTING!

Take your telescope into your backyard or a nearby park and look at the trees. Listen for birdsong or other noises that indicate where some wildlife might be hiding.

BIRDS

Passerine

Owl

If you spot a bird perching on a branch, take a look at its feet. Can you see how many toes it has? Which way do they point?

ANSWER: More than half of all the different kinds, or species, of birds are classed as passerines, or "perching birds." They have four toes on each foot: three pointing forward and one pointing backward. Some other birds that can perch, such as owls, have two toes pointing forward and two pointing backward.

SQUIRRELS

Squirrels love to move through trees, and they rarely sit still! If a squirrel is moving fast it will be tricky to follow with your telescope, but try to spot one climbing headfirst down a tree trunk. What do you notice about its hind legs?

ANSWER: Squirrels are one of the few mammals that can climb down headfirst. They do this by rotating their back ankles 180 degrees. This causes their feet to point backward so they can grip the tree bark with their claws.

Elephant bird

Big and Small

Bee hummingbird

The world's smallest bird is the bee hummingbird, which measures 2¼ inches long, including the bill and tail. The largest bird ever discovered was the flightless elephant bird of Madagascar, which became extinct about 1,000 years ago. It was nearly 10 feet tall!

CLOUD SURVEY

You don't have to look into space to find interesting things in the sky to spot with your telescope. Clouds are much closer to the ground, and there is so much to learn about them!

WHAT ARE CLOUDS?

Depending on the temperature, water can exist as a solid (ice), as a liquid, and as a gas called **water vapor**. The gas is invisible, but when there is a lot of it in the air we can sense it—the air will feel humid or muggy. When air rises higher, it cools down. Cool air can't hold as much water vapor as warm air can, so when there is too much water vapor for the air to hold, it **condenses** around little pieces of dust and becomes tiny droplets. Clouds are formed from billions of these droplets.

Q UICK FACT

During a storm, towering cumulonumbus clouds can grow more than 6 miles high. They typically produce periods of very heavy rain.

Cirrocumulus

HIGH LEVEL

TYPES OF CLOUDS

Meteorologists (scientists who study the weather), divide clouds into different types, based on their height and appearance. Low-level cumulus clouds are puffy and white, like cotton balls. Stratus clouds form flat layers. Cirrus clouds are thin and wispy. Many clouds are a mix of two or more types, such as cirrocumulus. These high clouds are made up of small, puffy cloudlets.

MID LEVEL

Stratocumulus

Cumulonimbus

LOW LEVEL

Cirrus

Cirrostratus

Altocumulus

Altostratus

Cumulus

Nimbostratus

Stratus

GET SPOTTING!

Astronomers don't usually like clouds because their telescopes can't see through them to study the space objects beyond. But why not have a look at the clouds themselves?

CLOUDS

Choose a cloud and try to identify it using the illustration on page 20. Now take a look at it with your telescope. Can you see any shadows or more detail in its structure?

How many additional details you can see will depend on how far away the clouds are. Low clouds may be just a few hundred feet above the ground. High clouds may be several miles up.

RAINBOWS

Next time you spot a rainbow in the sky, look at it through your telescope. Can you see a wider range of colors?

Rainbows form when sunlight is refracted as it passes through water droplets in the air. The white sunlight splits into the different colors of the spectrum, from red to violet.

Cloud Cover

Meteorologists are interested in how much of the sky is covered in clouds at any given time. They measure this using a unit called an **okta**. Imagine that the sky is divided into eight equal-size sections. If all the clouds in the sky were joined into one giant cloud, how many of these sections would they fill? A completely clear sky would be recorded as 0 oktas. A completely cloud-covered sky would be 8 oktas.

AWESOME ARCHITECTURE

Do you ever look up when you're out and about? Sometimes we're so focused on where we're going that we forget to really look at the buildings and structures around us.

SKYSCRAPERS

Some big cities are like forests, with skyscrapers soaring upward instead of trees. These towering buildings have only become possible in the last 150 years or so. Before that, big buildings were made from stone. Stone is too heavy to build really tall buildings—they would weigh so much that the supporting walls would collapse. But engineers figured out how to use strong but lightweight steel frames to build higher and higher. By 1900, there were skyscrapers 26 stories high, with taller ones being built each year.

ARCHITECTURE STYLES

Styles in architecture change just like clothing styles do. An office building built in the early 1900s will look different from one built in the 1960s. The older building may have ornate details, while a more modern building is sleek and streamlined. A building's style also has to do with its function—a cathedral will look different from an apartment building, and a house will look different from an office building.

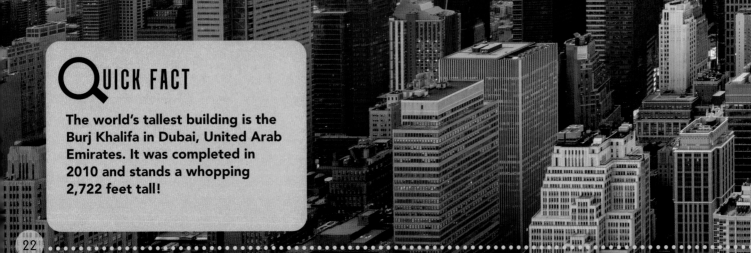

QUICK FACT

The world's tallest building is the Burj Khalifa in Dubai, United Arab Emirates. It was completed in 2010 and stands a whopping 2,722 feet tall!

GET SPOTTING!

Take your telescope out into a town or city and look up. You may be amazed by what you see! While using your telescope in public, be sure to mind people's privacy. It isn't polite to spy on people.

SKYSCRAPERS

If you can visit a city big enough to have skyscrapers, take a look at the upper floors. Can you see any details that are not visible from the ground?

You may be able to see carvings on older buildings or structural parts on newer buildings. Based on what you see, can you guess how old the buildings are?

GARGOYLES

Some old buildings have gargoyles on their upper sections. These are water spouts in the shape of animals or creatures. They allow water to flow off the roof and away from the sides of the building. Gargoyles are commonly found in Europe, but some American buildings, such as the Chrysler Building in New York City (above), have them, too.

CELL TOWERS

Cell phones rely on a network of antennae placed around a city. Some of them are stand-alone, but many are mounted on the roofs of tall buildings. What do they look like?

A cell tower usually has more than one bar-shaped antenna. How many antennae are there on the tower that you're looking at?

LOOKING DOWN

Is there a tall building near you where the public is allowed to go to the top? Or do you know someone who lives or works in a skyscraper? Use your telescope to look out of the window. How far can you see?

Depending on how high you are, you can probably see for at least several miles on a clear day. What details can you see on the ground?

SENDING SIGNALS

One of the earliest uses of the telescope was to help soldiers and sailors view far-off signals. Communicating with the rest of their force was often crucial in helping to win a battle, but in the days before telegraphs or telephones were invented, it was a real challenge.

SEMAPHORE

One way of communicating over long distances was to use **semaphore**. A person would spell out a message by waving two flags. Each position of the flags represented a different letter. Using a telescope, an observer a mile or more away could read the signals. In 1794, a French engineer invented the signal telegraph. This was a series of towers spaced several miles apart, with arms at the top. The arms could be moved into position to convey a message. An observer at the next tower would read the message and pass it along, and so on.

NAVAL FLAGS

Sailing ships ran strings of flags from their masts. Each flag had a different meaning, such as "ship on fire; keep clear" or "man overboard." The flags could also stand for letters to spell out a specific message. Warships often kept their flags' meanings secret. An observer on another ship would need to have the correct key to decode the message. Ships still use signal flags today.

GET SPOTTING!

You don't need to wait for a battle to use semaphore code! Work with a friend to develop your own code. It could use flags, hand signals, or something else entirely. Work out a way of showing different letters—you could learn the American Sign Language alphabet if you like. You can also invent signals to communicate a specific message, such as "let's get some food!"

TEST IT OUT

Find a large, open space such as a playing field. Stand at one end of the field with the telescope, and have a friend stand at the other end to signal a message. Watch carefully as they signal. Can you decipher the message?

One of the most common problems in semaphore is making a mistake and confusing the person you're signaling to. In the semaphore alphabet (right), there is a special signal that means "I made a mistake; ignore the previous signal." A signal like that may be very useful in your code, too!

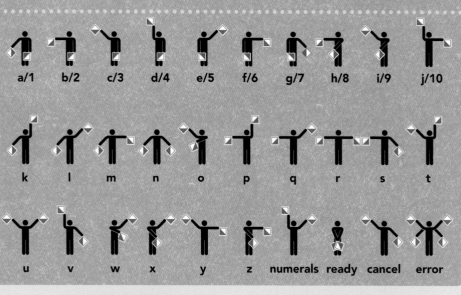

a/1 b/2 c/3 d/4 e/5 f/6 g/7 h/8 i/9 j/10

k l m n o p q r s t

u v w x y z numerals ready cancel error

QUICK FACT

The higher you are, the farther you can see. Ships often had a "crow's nest" at the top of the main mast. From here, a lookout with a telescope could get a great view of any other ships—or even spot land!

The Right to Be Blind

During the Battle of Copenhagen in 1801, the admiral in charge of the British fleet ran up a signal to order a retreat. One of his captains, Horatio Nelson, didn't want to retreat—he thought they could win. Nelson was blind in one eye, so he held his telescope to his bad eye and said, "I have a right to be blind sometimes…I really do not see the signal!" He kept fighting, and the British won the battle.

FLYING MACHINES

Who hasn't looked up at the sky and wished that they had the ability to fly? Long ago, a few brave souls tried making wings and jumping off a cliff or tall building—often with disastrous results. But engineers didn't give up on the idea and now, thanks to the invention of flying machines, humans can take to the air.

 UICK FACT

Some early airships replaced hot air with lightweight hydrogen gas, but they were very dangerous. Hydrogen burns easily, and a single spark could destroy an airship.

BALLOONS

The first flying craft to carry humans was the hot-air balloon. The Montgolfier brothers, who owned a paper factory in France, had observed that heated air could make a paper bag rise. They built a large balloon of fabric and paper and used fire to heat the air inside. In 1783, the first passengers were a sheep, a duck, and a rooster. About a month after their safe return, the brothers sent human passengers into the air for the first time.

THE FIRST AIRPLANES

Balloons had their limits. They were hard to steer, and having a fire on board was dangerous. Another pair of brothers, Wilbur and Orville Wright, experimented with a different type of machine. Their airplane had wings to provide lift, a motor to provide thrust, and a system for controlling its movement. They made their first successful flight in Kitty Hawk, North Carolina, in 1903.

GET SPOTTING!

Moving objects are not easy to follow with a telescope, but some flying machines move slowly enough that you should be able to get a good look at them.

AIRPLANES

The next time an airplane flies overhead, see if you can get a closer look. Can you see its engines?

Most passenger planes have jet engines under the wings. They take in air and burn it with fuel, creating a jet of hot gas that pushes the plane forward. Smaller airplanes have spinning propellers.

HOT-AIR BALLOON

You may be lucky enough to see a hot-air balloon. Can you tell how it is powered?

A hot-air balloon has a gas burner beneath the opening of the balloon. It's not on all the time, but the pilot gives the burner a blast when they need to go higher.

CONTRAILS

Use your telescope to examine the white trail left behind by a jet airplane. What do you think it is made of?

ANSWER: These white streams are called contrails. They form when hot, humid air from the jet engine mixes with the cooler air around it. The water vapor condenses into droplets—similar to the way a cloud forms.

Helicopters

Helicopters can take off into the air vertically, without needing a runway to build up speed. They do this thanks to a spinning rotor at the top. Most helicopters have a second rotor on the tail that keeps the whole thing from spinning in circles. In flight, the rotors spin too fast for you to see the individual blades.

ASTRONOMY BASICS

Ever since Galileo, astronomers have been using telescopes to get a better look at the objects in space. They have discovered new planets, stars, and **galaxies**. They have also learned a lot about the universe and how it works. Now it's your turn!

QUICK FACT

The stars are always shining. In fact, there are just as many stars in the daytime sky as there are at night—we just can't see them because the Sun's brightness drowns them out.

A WORLD OF TWO HALVES

Earth is a sphere with an imaginary line around the middle, like a belt, called the equator. The equator divides the planet into two halves called **hemispheres**. A person in the northern hemisphere sees a different section of the sky than a person in the southern hemisphere.

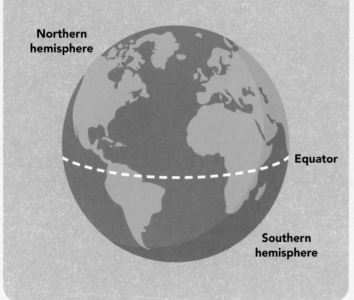

Northern hemisphere

Equator

Southern hemisphere

MOVING STARS

Our planet is constantly moving. Every day it spins once on its axis, causing day and night. It is day when your part of Earth is pointing toward the Sun, and night when it is pointing away from the Sun. Although the Sun appears to rise in the east, move across the sky, and then set in the west, it is actually staying still—it's the Earth that's spinning. This spinning also makes the stars appear to move across the night sky. If you watch the sky over a few hours, the stars will move from east to west.

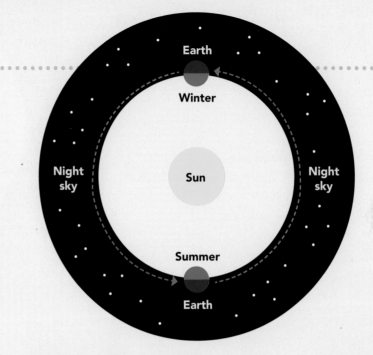

STARGAZING SEASON

Earth travels around the Sun in a big loop, called an orbit. This takes a whole year and causes the seasons. It also changes which stars are visible. In summer, the night side of Earth faces a completely different direction than it faces during the winter. This means that some stars and **constellations** that are visible in one season will disappear in another.

DIRECTIONS AND DEGREES

To find objects in the night sky, you need to know in which direction you are looking. A map or compass can tell you which way is north. You also need a way to measure the distance between objects. In math, a circle can be divided into 360 "slices" called degrees, and astronomers divide up the sky in the same way. You can use your fist to estimate degrees. Stand with your arm stretched out straight in the direction you want to look, and make your hand into a fist. The area of the sky covered by your fist, from left to right, is about 10 degrees.

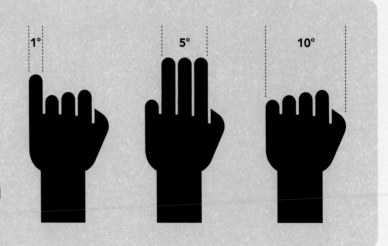

STARGAZING TIPS

Navigating the night sky is not always easy—it takes patience and practice. Here are some quick and easy tips to help you make the most of your stargazing sessions.

GO DARK

The darker the skies, the more you will see. Many distant space objects are very dim, so if there is a lot of other light (such as streetlights or lit buildings), it will drown out the stars. If you live in a big city, it's hard to avoid **light pollution**, but getting away from extra-bright lights will help a little.

AVOID THE MOON

If you want to see stars, you should pick a day when the Moon isn't too bright. A bright full moon can make dimmer objects impossible to see. The Moon rises and sets at different times throughout its cycle. About a week after the full moon is a good time to go stargazing because the Moon won't rise until late at night. These conditions will last until shortly after the new moon.

CHOOSE A SITE

In addition to finding a place without too much light pollution, think about how much of the sky you can see. If there are tall trees or buildings all around, you won't get a clear view of objects close to the **horizon**.

CHECK THE FORECAST

Clouds can spoil any stargazing trip by blocking your view of the sky. Other weather conditions can also affect how much you will see. Dry weather is better for stargazing, and there should be no haze in the air.

QUICK FACT

It takes your eyes time to adjust to the dark. The longer you stay in the dark, the more stars you will see—even just ten minutes will make a difference. Once your eyes have adjusted, keep them ready for stargazing by avoiding bright lights such as flashlights or phone screens.

CHECKLIST

Once you've chosen a good night to head out, make sure you have all the supplies you need. Here is a simple checklist of things to take:

- **A responsible adult**
- **Plenty of warm layers—it can get really cold at night!**
- **Your telescope and this book**
- **A notebook and pen to record what you see**
- **A red flashlight, or a regular flashlight covered in red cellophane (this will keep you from spoiling your night vision with bright white light)**
- **Snacks and drinks**
- **Sky maps, or a tablet, laptop, or cell phone with a stargazing app (set them in night mode to protect your night vision)**
- **A compass for finding direction**
- **A reclining chair, if you have one (lying down keeps your neck from getting too sore)**
- **A picnic blanket for lying on the ground**

THE SURFACE OF THE MOON

Crust

Mantle

Outer core

Partial melt

Inner core

Looking at the Moon is a great way to start your stargazing. In fact, you could spend a whole session just looking at the Moon! If you go out on a night when the Moon is full, you'll get a great view of it—though its light will make dimmer objects harder to see.

EARTH'S PARTNER

The Moon is held in orbit by Earth's **gravity**, making it our constant companion as we move through space. It spins on its own axis as it orbits Earth, so that the same half of it is always facing us. You won't be able to see the far side of the Moon through your telescope—only astronauts traveling around the Moon have ever seen it.

PLAINS AND CRATERS

Most of the space rocks on a collision course with Earth burn up in our atmosphere. The Moon doesn't have the same thick blanket of gases for protection, so it is often hit by **asteroids** and other rocks. This, along with the lack of erosion, means its surface is pockmarked by **craters** of various sizes. The dark areas on the Moon's surface are plains called **maria**. They were formed billions of years ago when large impact sites were filled with lava.

HOW IT FORMED

Scientists think that an object about the size of Mars collided with Earth 4.5 billion years ago. The impact hurled large amounts of debris and some of this clumped together to form the Moon. It was a molten mess at first, but it gradually cooled and hardened into a sphere with a hard outer crust and a mantle beneath. It has an iron **core**, just like Earth.

QUICK FACT

The term "maria" is the Latin word for "seas," but they are made of solidified lava, not water. There is no liquid water on the Moon.

GET SPOTTING!

You can use your telescope to get a closer look at some of the features on the Moon's surface.

APOLLO 17

APOLLO 15

Aristarchus

Copernicus

APOLLO 11

APOLLO 16

APOLLO 14

Kepler   APOLLO 12

Tycho

CRATERS

Use the map on the left to find and observe the craters known as Aristarchus, Copernicus, Kepler, and Tycho. What do they have in common?

ANSWER: They are surrounded by "rays" of lighter material, spreading out in all directions. The rays are formed from debris that was thrown up in the impact that formed the crater.

LANDING SITES

The map (left) also shows the landing sites of the six crewed missions to land on the Moon. Look at them on the Moon through your telescope. Why do you think they were chosen?

ANSWER: Scientists took many factors into account when choosing landing sites. One requirement was that they be fairly flat, with fewer boulders that could wreck the lander.

TAKE IT FARTHER

There are mountains nearly 1 mile high in the middle of the Copernicus crater. You may be able to see them with binoculars or a more powerful telescope.

THE CHANGING MOON

After the Sun, the Moon is the brightest object in the sky. That's pretty impressive when you realize that the Moon doesn't produce any of its own light! Instead, it reflects light from the Sun. But why does the Moon change shape from day to day?

PHASES OF THE MOON

Sometimes the Moon is directly between Earth and the Sun. Other times, it is on the far side from the Sun, or at a right angle. But half of the Moon—the half facing the Sun—is always brightly lit. Depending on the Moon's position, though, we may only see part of the bright side. It takes 28 days for the Moon to complete one orbit around the Earth, and during this cycle it goes from a full moon, gradually waning (getting smaller) to a crescent and then a new moon, then waxing (getting bigger) back to a full moon again. These are called phases.

LUNAR ECLIPSES

Every once in a while, the Moon, Earth, and the Sun line up perfectly, with Earth between the other two. Our planet blocks sunlight from reaching the Moon, causing a **lunar eclipse**. An eclipse can only happen during a full moon. The Moon will gradually fade away as Earth's shadow covers it. It will not go completely dark, because Earth's atmosphere refracts some of the sunlight onto the Moon, often making it appear reddish.

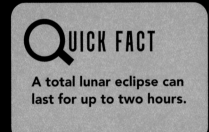

QUICK FACT

A total lunar eclipse can last for up to two hours.

GET SPOTTING!

There are interesting things to see on the Moon, no matter what phase it is in on the night you go stargazing. Looking at the Moon during different phases can reveal different areas and features.

ON THE EDGE

As long as the Moon is not completely full, there will be a line called the terminator, which separates the bright part of the Moon from the part that is in darkness. See if you can find it. Why do you think it might be a good place to look for craters?

ANSWER: Shadows are longer near the terminator, so it is easier to see the differences in height. This makes craters stand out more clearly.

ECLIPSES

Look online or use an app to find out when the next lunar eclipse will be, then take your telescope out to observe it. You'll see the Moon change color. Why do you think the color change takes a while to cover the full moon?

ANSWER: As the Moon and Earth move, it takes several minutes for them to get into a position where Earth completely blocks the Sun's light.

TAKE IT FARTHER

If you are looking at the right moment during an eclipse, you may see a blue or turquoise band at the edge of the shadow on the Moon. This is caused by light passing through the ozone layer in Earth's atmosphere. It blocks out red light and enhances blue light.

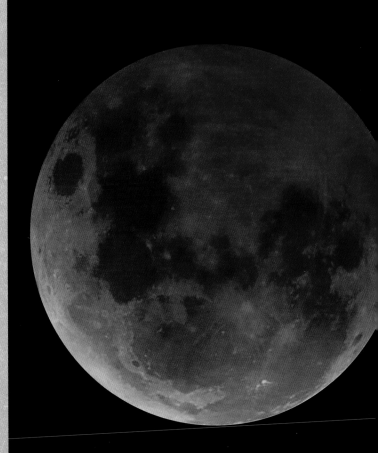

VENUS

Venus travels closer to Earth than any other planet. It is a rocky planet that is about the same size as Earth, but the similarities end there. While Earth has perfect conditions for life, Venus is incredibly deadly!

SCORCHING SURFACE

Venus is not the closest planet to the Sun, but it is the hottest. It is surrounded by thick clouds of carbon dioxide that trap the Sun's heat, creating a runaway greenhouse effect. Temperatures on the surface can reach 880°F! The **air pressure** is crushingly strong, and the atmosphere also holds clouds of deadly sulfuric acid. The few spacecraft that managed to land on Venus were quickly destroyed by the heat and pressure.

The Soviet Union sent more than ten unmanned missions to Venus, some of which reached the surface, before being destroyed.

 QUICK FACT

The thick clouds around Venus block a telescope's view. It is only fairly recently that spacecraft in orbit have been able to use radar to "see" through the clouds and produce detailed maps of the surface.

GET SPOTTING!

Finding planets in the night sky can be a bit tricky. From one night to the next, their position changes in relation to the stars. They often move from west to east, but sometimes they move east to west. You will need to check an astronomy website or app to find where to look for Venus on the night that you are observing. At some times during the year, it may not be visible at all.

Volcanoes and Craters

The craters on the surface of Venus are fairly large. That's because only the largest meteoroids can make it through the atmosphere without burning up before they hit the surface. Venus also has mountains and valleys, and thousands of volcanoes. Recent space missions have provided evidence that some of these volcanoes are still active.

GODDESS OF BEAUTY

Venus is always close to the Sun and it often appears either just before sunrise or just after sunset. The ancient Egyptians and Greeks called it the "morning star" and the "evening star," not realizing at first that the two were actually the same object. The Romans gave this bright white starlike object its current name after their goddess of beauty.

EVENING STAR

Choose a time when Venus is visible in the evening sky, looking very bright to the naked eye, and find it with your telescope. Why do you think it is often seen close to the Sun?

ANSWER: The orbit of Venus lies between Earth and the Sun, so it always appears close to the Sun. However, there are times when the Sun's light is so bright that it makes Venus impossible to see.

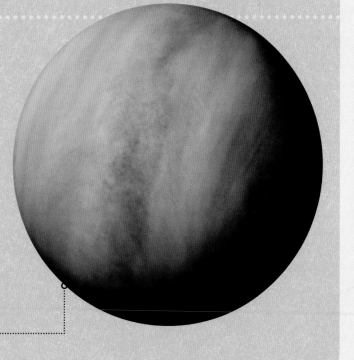

Venus is often the first bright object to appear in the sky after sunset.

TAKE IT FARTHER

Because Venus is between Earth and the Sun, from Earth it appears to have phases, like the Moon. You probably won't be able to see these with your telescope, but a slightly more powerful telescope will show Venus going from a crescent to a full disk and back again.

MARS

Mars is famous in science fiction as the source of Martian invaders that terrorize Earth. The stories may be made up, but this rocky planet is still a fascinating world. Recent discoveries have shown that it may have once been more like Earth.

NASA's *Curiosity* rover has been exploring the surface of Mars since 2012.

A WATERY WORLD?

Recent explorations by rovers on the surface of Mars have provided evidence that there may once have been water flowing on the planet's surface. It shaped the land and rocks in the same way that rivers erode land on Earth. The atmosphere of Mars is now so thin that any liquid water on the surface would **evaporate** away into space. But there is still some water, in the form of ice, beneath the surface and at the poles.

QUICK FACT

Scientists are working on ways for astronauts to travel to Mars. The trip would take about six months, but we don't have a way to send all the supplies that the astronauts would need for such a long voyage.

GET SPOTTING!

The distance from Earth to Mars varies a lot. Sometimes Mars is as close as 34 million miles—just over a third of the distance from Earth to the Sun. But when the planets' orbits take them to opposite sides of the Sun, Earth and Mars can be 250 million miles apart. When Mars is at its closest, it outshines the brightest star in the night sky. A website or app can tell you where to find Mars and how close it is to Earth.

SMALL AND ROCKY

Find Mars with the naked eye first. It looks like a bright star, but it is actually a rocky planet. It is also very small—just over half as wide as Earth, making it the second-smallest of the eight planets. If it is so small, why do you think it appears brighter than most stars?

ANSWER: Mars is much closer to us than any of the stars, so it appears bigger and brighter in comparison.

Ice Caps

Just like Earth, Mars has a surface marked with canyons and volcanoes, though it has more craters than our home planet. There is another similarity, too: Mars has ice caps at its north and south poles. They grow and shrink as the seasons change. Like Earth's ice caps, they are made of water, but the ones on Mars are covered with a skin of frozen carbon dioxide. This is the same material that we call dry ice, which can produce a swirling mist for special effects.

THE RED PLANET

Now look at Mars through your telescope. You won't be able to see any details on the surface, but its red color should stand out clearly. Do you know why Mars is this color?

ANSWER: The rocks and dust on the surface of Mars are made of iron-rich minerals that turn red as they oxidize, or rust.

TAKE IT FARTHER

Mars is small and far away, but with a more powerful telescope you might be able to see the ice caps at its poles.

JUPITER

Jupiter is the biggest planet in our solar system and it is bigger than all the other seven planets combined! It is truly king of the planets, just like Jupiter was king of the Roman gods. Its brightness and quick movement through the sky told ancient astronomers that this object was something special.

GAS GIANT

Unlike Earth, Venus, and Mars, Jupiter does not have a solid surface. Instead, it is made up of swirling clouds of hydrogen and helium. Deep below the surface, the intense pressure of the gases above turns some of the hydrogen into liquid, forming a giant ocean. There may be a core of solid material at the center, but astronomers aren't certain.

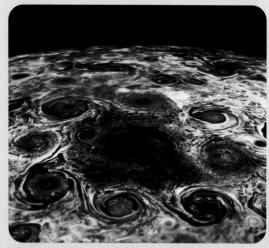

NASA captured this image showing swirling storms gathered around one of Jupiter's poles.

BANDS OF COLOR

Jupiter's surface appears to have stripes of different colors. These are clouds of water ice, ammonia, and other chemicals. Jupiter spins very quickly, which creates strong winds that separate the clouds into bands. The famous Great Red Spot is a storm around twice the size of Earth that has been raging for at least several hundred years! Jupiter is also surrounded by a faint system of rings, which were discovered in 1979. They are dark and very difficult to see.

JUPITER'S MOONS

Galileo discovered Jupiter's four largest moons—Ganymede, Callisto, Io, and Europa—in 1610. They are called the "Galilean moons" in his honor. Since then, astronomers have used powerful telescopes to find at least 70 more. There are probably still more to be found. Jupiter's powerful gravity holds all these moons in orbit. There is evidence that some of the larger moons have liquid water beneath their surface, raising the possibility that they may harbor life.

GET SPOTTING!

Jupiter is one of the brightest objects in the sky (as in the image (right) next to the Moon). Roughly once a year it will be "in opposition" to Earth—the two planets will be aligned and Jupiter will be at its closest point. This is the best time to observe Jupiter, even though it will be visible on most other nights.

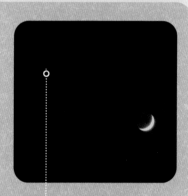

Jupiter

FINDING MOONS

Find Jupiter's location using an app or website and look at it through your telescope. If you hold it really steady you might see four pinpricks of light surrounding the planet, arranged roughly in a line. These are the Galilean moons. Sometimes only three moons are visible. Do you know why this is?

ANSWER: The moons travel around Jupiter, just like our own moon orbits Earth. If one of the moons is traveling behind Jupiter while you are observing, you won't be able to see it.

TAKE IT FARTHER

A more powerful telescope may be able to show you the stripes of clouds and even the Great Red Spot, as long as it is on the side of the planet facing you.

WHAT ARE STARS?

Like our Sun, stars are giant balls of glowing gas. Stars are mainly made up of **hydrogen** and helium. Deep inside a star's core, a **nuclear reaction** takes place that turns hydrogen into helium. This process releases large amounts of energy, producing the heat and light that we depend on.

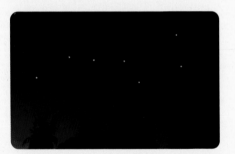

CONSTELLATIONS

Humans have been finding patterns in the stars for thousands of years. We give these patterns names to describe shapes that they seem to form. One of the most famous of all of these is the Big Dipper (above). Large groups of stars that form a shape are called constellations. Over the centuries, astronomers in different countries have named hundreds of constellations. Today, astronomers have agreed to recognize 88 main constellations. Together, these constellations cover the entire night sky. However, the Big Dipper is not a constellation. It is a smaller grouping called an **asterism**, which makes up part of the constellation Ursa Major.

Imaginary lines join the stars together to form the northern constellation Ursa Major, also known as the Great Bear. The part known as the Big Dipper is shown here using red lines.

GET SPOTTING!

Ursa Major is the third-largest of the 88 constellations, but most of its stars are fairly dim. The seven stars that make up the Big Dipper are bright and easy to see. The Big Dipper is visible year-round from most places in the northern hemisphere and will always lie roughly north, although at times it will be low and close to the horizon. It can be seen from parts of the southern hemisphere some of the time.

DOUBLE STAR

Four stars make up the scoop part of the Big Dipper, with three more making up the handle. Find the middle star of the handle—the one second in from the end—and take a closer look with your telescope. What do you see?

ANSWER: This bright star is called Mizar, and it's hiding a surprise: a dimmer star called Alcor tucked in next to it. Astronomers have recently discovered that Mizar is actually a system of four stars that are so close together that we can't tell them apart, and Alcor is another pair of stars. These six stars are all held in place by each other's gravity.

Light Years

The stars that make up the constellations are not necessarily near each other in space. The closest of the stars in the Big Dipper is about 78 light years from Earth. This means that the light it produces takes 78 years to reach us! Compared to light from the Sun, which takes about 8 minutes to reach us, that is a very long time. The other stars in the asterism are even farther away. The farthest is 123 light years from Earth.

QUICK FACT

People in other countries have different names for the Big Dipper. They include the Plough, the Saucepan, the Great Wagon, and the Bucket.

STAR MAPS

Because Earth is round, only half the sky is visible from your position. From the southern hemisphere you see stars that are never visible from the north, and vice versa. To chart the night sky we need two maps—one for the north and one for the south.

Aquarius
Pisces
Pegasus
Cetus
Equuleus
Aries
Lacerta
Andromeda
Triangulum
Delphinus
Cassiopeia
Taurus
Aquila
Perseus
Sagitta
Cygnus
Cepheus
Serpens
Polaris
Auriga
Ophiuchus
Cameleopardalis
Orion
Draco
Ursa Minor
Hercules
Gemini
Corona Borealis
Lynx
Canis Minor
Serpens
Ursa Major
Leo Minor
Cancer
Canes Venatici
Boötes
Leo
Coma Berenices
Hydra
Virgo

NORTHERN HEMISPHERE

NORTHERN SKIES

This map is most accurate for the North Pole, when you would see the bright star Polaris straight above your head. The map's edges represent the horizon. There are no directions marked, because they change with the seasons. For example, in January, Hercules will be on the northern horizon, but in April it will be in the east.

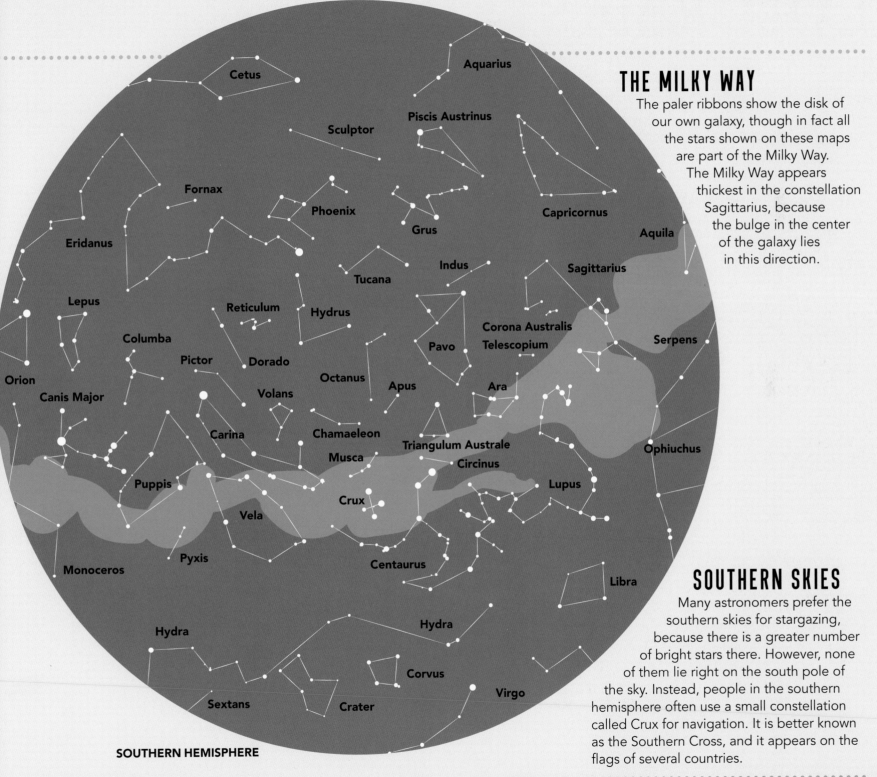

THE MILKY WAY

The paler ribbons show the disk of our own galaxy, though in fact all the stars shown on these maps are part of the Milky Way. The Milky Way appears thickest in the constellation Sagittarius, because the bulge in the center of the galaxy lies in this direction.

SOUTHERN SKIES

Many astronomers prefer the southern skies for stargazing, because there is a greater number of bright stars there. However, none of them lie right on the south pole of the sky. Instead, people in the southern hemisphere often use a small constellation called Crux for navigation. It is better known as the Southern Cross, and it appears on the flags of several countries.

SOUTHERN HEMISPHERE

Cetus
Aquarius
Piscis Austrinus
Sculptor
Fornax
Phoenix
Capricornus
Grus
Aquila
Eridanus
Tucana
Indus
Sagittarius
Lepus
Reticulum
Hydrus
Corona Australis
Serpens
Columba
Pavo
Telescopium
Pictor
Dorado
Octanus
Apus
Ara
Orion
Volans
Ophiuchus
Canis Major
Chamaeleon
Triangulum Australe
Carina
Musca
Circinus
Lupus
Crux
Puppis
Vela
Centaurus
Libra
Pyxis
Monoceros
Hydra
Hydra
Corvus
Virgo
Sextans
Crater

COLORED STARS

Stars may all look more or less the same to us, but they're not. Some are small, some are medium-sized, and others are truly enormous. Some shine brightly, while others are dimmer. Stars even come in different colors!

THE BIRTH OF A STAR

Stars are not living things, but they go through a series of stages called a life cycle. They begin as swirling clumps of gas and dust, held together by gravity. If there is enough mass in the star, it will heat up and a nuclear reaction will begin in its core, making it light up. Once this happens, the star becomes a "main sequence star."

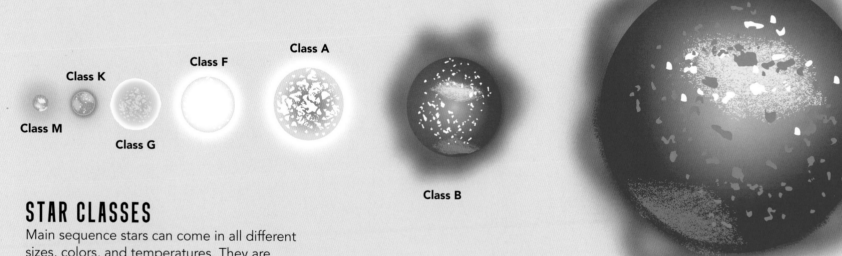

Class M

Class K

Class G

Class F

Class A

Class B

Class O

STAR CLASSES

Main sequence stars can come in all different sizes, colors, and temperatures. They are often put into one of seven groups (O, B, A, F, G, K, and M) based on their temperature. O stars, which appear blue, are the hottest and M stars, which appear red, are the coolest. The hottest stars are usually also the biggest.

GET SPOTTING!

The constellation Orion is easy to spot, though it is only visible in winter in the northern hemisphere and in summer in the southern hemisphere. It is named for a hunter in Greek mythology. Four bright stars make up his shoulders and feet, while another three in a row form his belt.

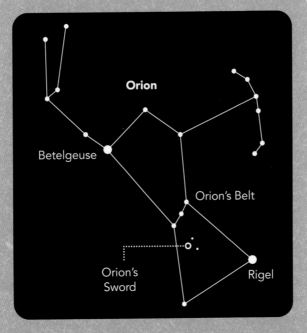

Orion

Betelgeuse

Orion's Belt

Orion's Sword

Rigel

BETELGEUSE

Find the star in Orion that appears in the upper left (in the northern hemisphere), representing his shoulder. This star is called Betelgeuse. What does it look like through your telescope?

Betelgeuse is a giant red star, so it appears reddish. It is nearing the end of its life and has swelled up to an enormous size, and will eventually explode.

RIGEL

Now find the star that appears in the lower right (in the northern hemisphere), representing Orion's foot. This star is called Rigel. What does it look like?

Rigel looks blue. It is a blue supergiant, many times larger than the Sun. Rigel is much younger than Betelgeuse, but burns hot and fast. It is probably also nearing the end of its life.

Death of a Star

As they burn, stars use up their hydrogen "fuel." Cooler stars burn slowly and will last for billions of years. Big, hot stars burn through their fuel at an astounding rate and may only last for a few million years. When the fuel is gone, a star will swell up, cool down, and turn red. After that, a small star will collapse and eventually stop glowing. A big star will explode in an event called a **supernova**.

TAKE IT FARTHER

Use a map or app to help you find colored stars, such as the red stars Antares and Aldebaran, in other constellations.

NEBULAE

The stars in the constellations may differ in size and color, but they do have one thing in common: each one formed inside a **nebula**. There are millions of these clouds of gas and dust in space, and they are a fascinating target for an astronomer.

EMPTY SPACE?

The space between stars is not completely empty. Atoms and other particles are spread very thinly though this space, which is called the interstellar medium (ISM). Most of it is hydrogen, with about a quarter helium and small quantities of dust. Gravity attracts all these particles to each other, and they can eventually come together to form clouds.

MESSIER NUMBERS

In the 1700s, a French astronomer named Charles Messier was on the hunt for **comets**. As he searched the sky, he made a list of fuzzy objects that were not comets, to help other astronomers avoid confusion. By 1783, he had a list of 110 objects, numbered in the order that he found them. Some of these "Messier objects" are nebulae, while others are galaxies or **star clusters**. Astronomers still refer to them by these numbers, such as M1 or M42.

INSIDE A NEBULA

Some nebulae are like nurseries where stars are born. Gravity slowly pulls together clumps of gas and dust. As the clumps grow, so does the strength of their gravity, attracting more material. They get bigger and bigger until they collapse. The material at the center of this collapsed region begins to heat up, forming a star. As the star attracts more material, it grows and becomes hotter.

QUICK FACT

The name "nebula" comes from the Latin word for "cloud."

GET SPOTTING!

Some nebulae are close enough to nearby stars that they glow. Other nebulae are dark and virtually impossible to spot. Here are two that you should be able to find fairly easily.

THE ORION NEBULA

There is a short row of stars in Orion that are positioned like a sword hanging from his belt. The second from the bottom may look a bit fuzzy. Take a closer look with your telescope. What do you see?

This "star" is actually the Orion Nebula (also called M42), which is about 24 light years across.

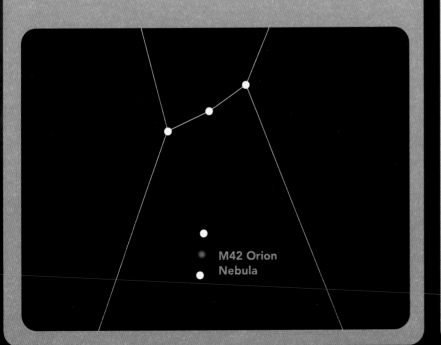

M42 Orion Nebula

TAKE IT FARTHER

With binoculars or a bigger telescope, on a dark night you should be able to see the Crab Nebula (M1, below) in the constellation Taurus. This nebula is the remains of a supernova that was seen on Earth in 1054. It was so bright that it was visible during the day!

In the summer, from the northern hemisphere you might also be able to see the Lagoon Nebula. This nebula is in the constellation Sagittarius. The central part of Sagittarius is an asterism that looks like a teapot. Following an imaginary line going from the top of the teapot's handle and through the star at the top of the lid will lead you to a fuzzy patch—this is the Lagoon Nebula.

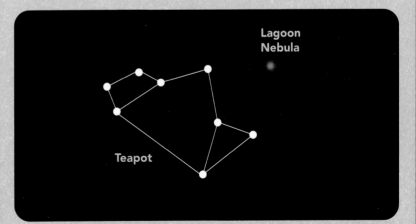

Lagoon Nebula

Teapot

The Lagoon Nebula (M8) was discovered in the 1600s and is a region of space where lots of stars are being born.

THE MILKY WAY

Most stars are part of a grouping called a galaxy. There are many billions of galaxies in the universe, each containing many billions of stars. The Sun is part of a galaxy called the Milky Way.

HOLDING TOGETHER

The force of gravity holds galaxies together. Every object with mass exerts a pull on other objects with mass, and this is what happens inside a galaxy. Galaxies are more than just stars. Many of the stars have planets orbiting them, and moons orbiting the planets. There are also nebulae in the spaces between the stars. Many galaxies, including ours, have an enormous black hole at the center. It exerts a huge gravitational force.

 QUICK FACT

The word "galaxy" comes from the ancient Greek name for the Milky Way. They called it *galaxias kyklos*, which means "milky circle."

GALAXY SHAPES

Not all galaxies are the same. Many of them are arranged in a flat spiral shape, with the stars in curved arms that make them look like a pinwheel. Others have a bar across the center, with spiral arms extending from its ends. Elliptical galaxies are smooth and oval shaped. Galaxies with no recognizable shape are called irregular galaxies.

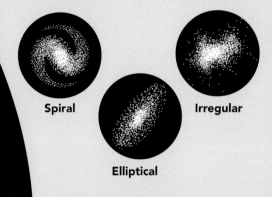

Spiral

Elliptical

Irregular

THE MILKY WAY

The Milky Way is a spiral galaxy, and the Sun and our solar system are located on one of its spiral arms. All the stars that you see in the night sky are part of the Milky Way. A few distant galaxies are visible as smudges. Powerful space telescopes, such as Hubble, have discovered countless other galaxies in deep space.

UICK FACT

Other cultures have different names for the Milky Way. Thanks to its white appearance, many of those names reference milk. Other names include "the snake of the skies," "the road to Santiago," "the way of birds," and "the route of scattered straw."

GET SPOTTING!

Any time you look at the stars, you are looking at part of the Milky Way. But to see the galaxy in all its glory, you will need a clear night and dark skies. It is difficult to see the Milky Way if you are in a city. But from the right location, it is visible as it streams across the sky.

THE MILKY WAY

You won't need your telescope to see the Milky Way, but it might be interesting to use it to explore some of the light and dark patches. The Milky Way travels in a wide band across the sky. Why do you think it has this shape instead of covering the entire sky?

ANSWER: Our galaxy is in the shape of a flat spiral. Imagine it as a pancake or hamburger patty. We are at a point about halfway between the center and the edge. If you look directly up or down, you'll be looking into the empty space beyond the Milky Way. But if you look to the side, you'll see an arc of stars. This is why the Milky Way looks like a stripe in the sky—we are looking at it from inside.

ANDROMEDA

Until about 100 years ago, astronomers thought that the stars in the Milky Way made up the entire universe. They had no idea that there were galaxies other than our own. Now we know that the universe is vaster than we ever could have imagined, with countless galaxies in all directions.

DISCOVERING GALAXIES

In the 1920s, the American astronomer Edwin Hubble was observing a fuzzy object known as the Andromeda Nebula, or M31. At the time, other astronomers believed it was a cloud of gas and dust. Hubble studied the stars that he could see inside M31 and realized that he could use their brightness as a way of calculating how far away they were. He discovered that M31 was much farther away than the most distant stars in the Milky Way. It wasn't a nebula at all—it was another galaxy!

AN EXPANDING UNIVERSE

Hubble's discovery completely changed everything we thought we knew about the universe. He and other astronomers soon discovered other galaxies beyond the boundaries of the Milky Way. Soon Hubble realized that all of these new galaxies were moving away from us. The farther they were, the faster they moved. This showed that the universe is expanding.

The 100-inch Hooker Telescope was used by Hubble.

QUICK FACT

It is difficult to accurately measure how far away distant objects are. Hubble estimated that Andromeda was about 1.5 million light years away, but astronomers now think the true figure is about 2.5 million light years.

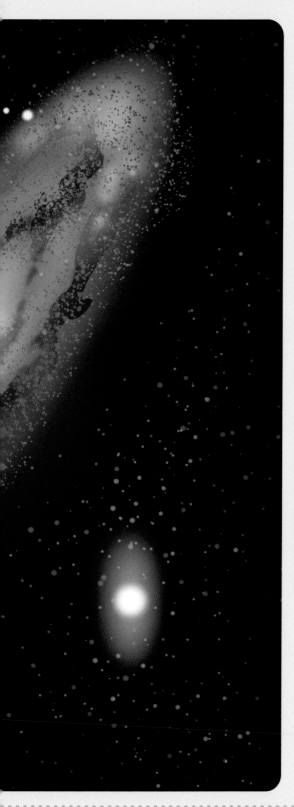

GET SPOTTING!

Fall is the best season for observing the Andromeda Galaxy in the northern hemisphere, since it will be high enough in the sky to be visible all night long. Start by finding the Big Dipper and follow it across the sky, past Polaris, and on to Cassiopeia, a constellation that looks like an "M" or a "W." Its deeper V shape is like an arrow that points to Andromeda.

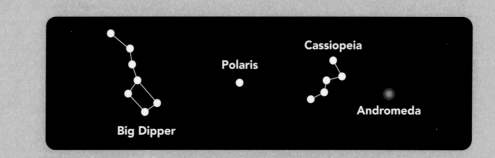

M32

Look at Andromeda with just your eyes first. It should look like a large, faint smudge of light, about as wide as a full moon. Now look at it with the telescope. What happens?

ANSWER: You may not see much of anything! Andromeda is visible to the naked eye because it is big, not because it is bright. The telescope reduces the contrast you can see. Andromeda is best viewed without a telescope. Try looking for M32 without your telescope, one of its companion galaxies that is found to the south. It is compact, more like a star in appearance, and is fairly bright.

Collision Course

All galaxies are moving, and that includes the Milky Way and Andromeda, one of our nearest galactic neighbors. In fact, the two galaxies are moving toward each other! Andromeda is traveling toward us at a speed of about 68 miles per second. In about 4.5 billion years, they will collide and merge.

TAKE IT FARTHER

See if you can find the Whirlpool Galaxy, also known as M51. It is below the last star in the handle of the Big Dipper. You may need binoculars or a more powerful telescope to see it.

STAR CLUSTERS

Galaxies contain billions of stars, but within them are smaller groupings called star clusters. The stars in these clusters are held together by each other's gravity. Unlike the stars in a constellation, the stars in a cluster are actually close to each other in space.

TYPES OF CLUSTERS

Star clusters can be divided into two types: open and globular. Some open clusters have just a dozen or so stars, while others have hundreds. The stars are not arranged in any type of pattern. A globular cluster has more stars—anywhere from thousands to hundreds of thousands. They are usually older than open clusters, and the stars are closely packed in a pattern that is roughly the shape of a sphere.

Open cluster

Globular cluster

QUICK FACT

Some of the stars in the largest globular clusters formed early in the Milky Way's history. These clusters contain stars that may be 12 or 13 billion years old—almost as old as the universe itself!

LEARNING FROM CLUSTERS

The stars in a cluster formed together at the same time, inside a nebula. However, the stars may be of different sizes and types, and some may burn through their fuel faster than others. Star clusters are useful for astronomers to study because the stars in them are roughly the same age and were created from the same material, but many of them have now moved into different stages of their life cycle. This has helped astronomers understand more about how stars change as they age.

GET SPOTTING!

Some star clusters are visible to the naked eye, while others are harder to spot.
Most of them are fairly dim, so you'll need a dark, clear night to spot them.

THE PLEIADES

The Pleiades (M45) form an open cluster that is easily visible in the fall and winter in the northern hemisphere. Follow the line of Orion's belt to the right, past the red star Aldebaran, until you see a fuzzy patch. What does it look like through your telescope?

ANSWER: On a clear night you can see six or seven stars with the naked eye, but with a telescope you should be able to see more! The stars in the Pleiades are all of a similar brightness and age.

THE HYADES

In the spring in the northern hemisphere, look for another open cluster called the Hyades. If you can find Aldebaran, look for the other stars making up the head of the bull in Taurus. The stars of the Hyades fill in its "face."

TAKE IT FARTHER

With a more powerful telescope, you can find the Great Globular Cluster, formally known as M13. This star cluster is made up of hundreds of thousands of stars—very different from the small open cluster of the Pleiades. M13 is best seen from the northern hemisphere in the fall. Use your star map to find the dim constellation of Hercules, then look between Hercules's shoulders to find the cluster.

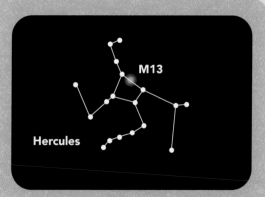

COMETS

Comets are rare but impressive visitors to our part of the solar system. As they near the Sun, these icy bodies produce spectacular "tails" that stream out from them.

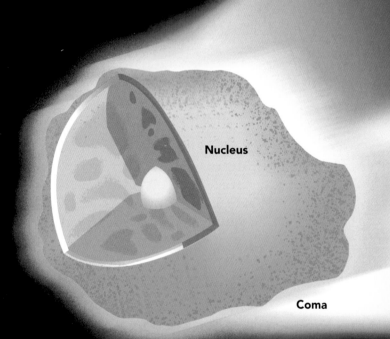

Gas tail ....o

THE OORT CLOUD

Many comets come from a region called the Oort Cloud, a spherical cloud of objects that starts far past the orbit of Neptune. Comets travel in loops around the Sun, like Earth does. But while a planet's orbit follows a roughly circular shape, a comet's orbit is very long and thin. It can take millions of years to travel from the Oort Cloud to the center of the solar system. The comet loops around the Sun and then heads back to where it came from.

Nucleus

Coma

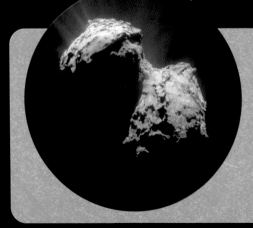

DIRTY SNOWBALLS

A comet's main body, called the nucleus, is a lump of rock and ice, often a few miles or less in diameter. As a comet gets closer to the Sun, it warms up. The ice turns into gas and forms an atmosphere called a coma around the nucleus. The wave of particles traveling out from the Sun pushes the coma out into a long tail. Sometimes you can see two separate tails—one made of dust and one of gas.

STUDYING COMETS

Comets are leftovers from the time when our solar system first formed. They may be the source of some of the water or chemicals on Earth. Scientists have sent many spacecraft to study comets. One brought back samples from a comet's tail. Another crashed deliberately into a comet's nucleus to learn more about it. One sent down a smaller craft to land on the comet's surface.

Dust tail

GET SPOTTING!

Unlike the stars, which are always there, comets are rarely visible. They are too small to see unless they are fairly close. Occasionally, one comes close enough to be viewed as a fuzzy blob through binoculars. It is even rarer for one to come close enough to be visible with the naked eye. These can be a spectacular sight, moving slowly across the sky for weeks or even months.

FINDING A COMET

Some comets pass by Earth on a regular schedule, such as Halley's Comet, which appears every 76 years. But most of them are only discovered shortly before they become visible. You'll need to check astronomy websites to see if there are any comets approaching. If you are lucky enough to see one, take a look at its long tail. Do you think it is traveling in front of the comet or streaming out behind?

ANSWER: It depends on which way the comet is traveling! A comet's tail always points away from the Sun. When a comet is traveling toward the Sun, the tail will stream out behind it. When it is moving away from the Sun, its tail is pushed out in front of it.

THE INTERNATIONAL SPACE STATION

The last target in space for you to find with your telescope is also the closest. The International Space Station (ISS) is a flying laboratory where astronauts from around the world live and work. When it is directly overhead, it is only about 250 miles away!

BUILDING A SPACE STATION

The different parts, or modules, of the space station were sent up, one by one, then assembled in space. The first modules were launched in 1998, and by 2000 the ISS was able to house astronauts. Since then, the ISS has expanded as more parts have been added. It is now about the size of a football field. It has living modules and laboratories, as well as solar panels to provide electricity. Spacecraft can dock to the ISS to transport astronauts or deliver supplies.

LIFE ON BOARD

Most astronauts stay on board for about six months. The ISS has everything they need—except gravity! Because of the station's orbit around Earth, people and objects inside float around weightlessly. They use handles to pull themselves along, and plenty of Velcro to keep everything secure. At night, they zip themselves into sleeping bags attached to the wall. They have to be careful with water and food, since tiny crumbs and droplets could float into the equipment and cause damage.

Science in Space

Astronauts on the ISS conduct experiments that can't be done on Earth's surface. Many of these depend on the effect of weightlessness. Astronauts study how space travel affects the human body, as well as its effect on plants and materials. They are also able to use their vantage point to gather information about glaciers, cities, and other features on Earth's surface.

GET SPOTTING!

hough the ISS is small, it's close enough and bright enough that at night s easy to see with the naked eye as it moves across the sky. It will only be le for a few minutes before it drops below the horizon again, so you need know exactly where and when to look. An astronomy app or website will give you the schedule for the next few weeks.

STATION SPOTTING

The ISS reflects sunlight and is usually fairly bright—sometimes as bright as Venus. It looks like an airplane, but it has no blinking or colored lights. Because it moves fairly quickly, it is easiest to track its path with just your eyes, but you can try following it with your telescope. In which direction is it traveling?

ANSWER: The ISS always appears in the west and travels east across the sky. It takes about 90 minutes for it to make one complete loop around Earth, so you can sometimes see it more than once per night.

QUICK FACT

The longest stay on the International Space Station was by Scott Kelly and Mikhail Kornienko, who stayed there for 340 days in 2015 and 2016.

TAKING IT FARTHER

With your telescope, you've spotted birds, clouds, signals, planets, stars, and even the International Space Station. But what if you want to see even more? A bigger telescope will show you more objects and more detail. Here are some tips on choosing one.

BINOCULARS

Many experienced stargazers say that binoculars are the best tool for beginners. Unless you get really fancy ones, binoculars are usually cheaper than a telescope. They're portable and easy to use. They also have a wider field of a vision than a telescope. For some objects that appear large in the sky, such as Andromeda or a star cluster, this can be a real positive. You would only be able to see part of the object through a powerful telescope.

SIZE AND STRENGTH

Binoculars are graded with a pair of numbers, such as 8 x 40. The first number is the magnification, so in this case the object you are viewing will appear eight times bigger than it would to the naked eye. The second number gives the width (in millimeters) of the big lenses at the front. The wider the lens, the more light the binoculars can collect from distant objects. However, lenses more than 50 mm wide will make the binoculars heavy and difficult to hold steady.

QUICK FACT

The objects in the solar system visible through medium-size binoculars include the outer planets Uranus and Neptune; Saturn's largest moon, Titan; and Jupiter's four Galilean moons.

Most telescopes include a smaller scope called a finder scope. It shows a wider area of sky than the main scope, and it helps you zero in on what you want to look at. Some telescopes use a red dot finder instead, which superimposes a red dot on the sky to help you aim.

You'll need a mount to hold the telescope steady. These are often shaped like a tripod. A type of mount called an altitude-azimuth mount will allow you to easily move the telescope up and down or side to side.

TELESCOPES

The telescope included with this book is a refracting telescope. You can buy bigger, more powerful versions of this basic design, but many beginner astronomers like to use a reflecting telescope.

The eyepiece controls the magnification. Some telescopes have an eyepiece permanently attached, but a telescope where you can swap out eyepieces gives you more flexibility. You may not always want the highest magnification possible.

ASK THE EXPERTS!

Find out if there is a local amateur astronomy society where you live. This is a great way to meet people who are interested in stargazing. They often hold open evenings where you can try out their telescopes. You can see what styles and models you like, and get an idea of what you'll be able to see with them. The society members can probably give you useful advice on choosing what to buy.

GLOSSARY

AIR PRESSURE
The pressing force of the weight of air on an object

APERTURE
The diameter of the light-collecting region of a telescope

ASTERISM
A group of stars that appears to form a shape when viewed from Earth, but that is not one of the agreed 88 constellations

ASTEROID
A small rocky body; most asteroids are in orbit in the asteroid belt, which is found between Mars and Jupiter

ASTRONOMER
A person who studies planets, stars, and other objects in space

ATMOSPHERE
Mass of gases surrounding some planets or moons

COMET
A celestial body made of ice and dust that develops a cloudy tail as it orbits closer to the Sun

CONCAVE
A lens shape that is curved so that it is thicker at the edges than in the middle

CONDENSE
To turn from a gas into a liquid

CONSTELLATION
A group of stars that form a pattern in the night sky

CONVEX
A curved lens shape that is thicker in the middle than at the edges

CORE
The center and hottest part of a planet, moon, or some asteroids

CRATERS
Large dents on the surface of a planet or moon made by a meteorite or other object

EVAPORATE
To turn from a liquid into a gas

EYEPIECE
Part of a reflecting telescope that you look into; or the smaller of the two lenses in a reflecting telescope

GALAXY
A massive group of stars, planets, gas, and dust

GRAVITY
A force that attracts objects with mass to each other

HEMISPHERE
One of two halves of the Earth; different stars are visible from the northern and the southern hemispheres

HORIZON
The place in the distance where the sky meets the land, from the point of view of an observer

HYDROGEN
A lightweight gas that is found in stars and was used in the past to make some types of airships fly

LENS
A piece of clear glass or plastic that has been ground into a curved shape to bend light

LIGHT POLLUTION
When electric lights in towns and cities make the sky brighter at night, making it hard to see stars

LUNAR ECLIPSE
An event during which Earth passes directly between the Sun and the Moon, blocking sunlight from reaching the Moon and casting a shadow

MARIA
Dark plains on the Moon, which were formed by ancient volcanic eruptions

MOON
An object that orbits a planet or asteroid

NEBULA
A massive cloud of dust and gas in space

NUCLEAR REACTION
A process in which the nucleus of an atom is changed by being split or by being joined to another nucleus

OBSERVATORY
A building that houses telescopes for observing the sky

OKTA
A unit of measurement for the amount of cloud cover in the sky; 0 okta is a completely clear sky; 8 okta is total cloud cover

ORBIT
The path of a planet, moon, comet, or spacecraft around another body

RADAR
A device that sends out radio waves and, based on the waves' reflection, can find out the position and speed of an object

REFLECTING TELESCOPE
A type of telescope that takes in light through a wide opening and uses a mirror to reflect the image into an eyepiece

REFRACTION
Bending of light as it passes from one medium to another, such as from air to glass

SEMAPHORE
A system of signaling using flags, poles, or body parts

STAR CLUSTER
A small group of stars held in position by each other's gravity

SUPERNOVA
The explosion of a very large star that gives off massive amounts of energy

WATER VAPOR
Water in the form of a gas

WAVELENGTH
The distance between one peak and the next along a wave such as a wave of light